W9-BZX-314

ROBOTS AND ROBOTICS

How Robots Work

Tony Hyland

A⁺

Smart Apple Media

This edition first published in 2008 in the United States of America by Smart Apple Media.
Reprinted 2007, 2008

Smart Apple Media
2140 Howard Drive West
North Mankato, Minnesota 56003

First published in 2007 by
MACMILLAN EDUCATION AUSTRALIA PTY LTD
15–19 Claremont Street, South Yarra, Australia 3141

Visit our Web site at www.macmillan.com.au or go directly to www.macmillanlibrary.com.au

Associated companies and representatives throughout the world.

Library of Congress Cataloging-in-Publication Data

Hyland, Tony.
  How robots work / by Tony Hyland.
    p. cm. — (Robots and robotics)
  Includes index.
  ISBN 978-1-59920-116-0
  1. Robots—Juvenile literature. 2. Robotics—Juvenile literature. I. Title.

  TJ211.2.H54 2007
  629.8'92—dc22

                                                                        2007004662

Edited by Margaret Maher
Text and cover design by Ivan Finnegan, iF Design
Page layout by Ivan Finnegan, iF Design
Photo research by Legend Images

Printed in U.S.

Acknowledgements
The author and the publisher are grateful to the following for permission to reproduce copyright material:

Front cover photograph: Qrio robots courtesy Yoshikazu Tsuno/AFP/Getty Images.

Photos courtesy of:
© Webking/Dreamstime.com, p. 26; Yoshikazu Tsuno/AFP/Getty Images, pp. 1, 23; Getty Images/James Porto, p. 28; Gottwald Port Technology GmbH, p. 25; Hanson Robotics, p. 21; © 2007 Honda Motor Company, pp. 4, 22; LIS – EPFL, Swarm-bots project, p. 15; Movie Store Collection Ltd, p. 29; NASA/JPL/Cornell University, p. 10; NOAA, p. 7; Photolibrary/Adam Hart-Davis/Science Photo Library, p. 13; Photolibrary/Maximilian Stock Ltd/Science Photo Library, pp. 9, 24; Photolibrary/Peter Menzel/Science Photo Library, pp. 12, 19, 20; Photolibrary/David Parker/Science Photo Library, p. 8; Photolibrary/Sam Ogden/Science Photo Library, p. 18; Photolibrary/Rosenfeld Images Ltd/Science Photo Library, p. 6; Photolibrary/Volker Steger/Science Photo Library, p. 5; Richard Greenhill Photo Library, pp. 14 (bottom), 16; © The RoboCup Federation, pp. 14 (top), 27; Andy Russell, p. 17; U.S. Navy, MC2 Elizabeth R. Allen, p. 11.

Background textures courtesy of Photodisc.

While every care has been taken to trace and acknowledge copyright, the publisher tenders their apologies for any accidental infringement where copyright has proved untraceable. Where the attempt has been unsuccessful, the publisher welcomes information that would redress the situation.

Contents

GLOSSARY WORDS
When a word is printed in **bold**, you can look up its meaning in the glossary on page 31.

Robots

There are more and more robots in the world. Once they were just figments of the imagination, metal creatures that clanked through old **science fiction** movies and books. Robots today are real, and you will find them in the most surprising places. Some are tiny, no bigger than a fly. Others are among the largest machines on Earth.

Robots are machines that can move and think for themselves. Most robots work in factories, doing endless, repeated tasks faster than any human. Other robots explore places that humans cannot safely reach. Some robots go to the bottom of the sea. Others go to the rocky surface of Mars.

There are also **surgical robots**, robots that carry out scientific experiments, and robots that **disarm** bombs. Today's toys often include robot technology—you can even **program** your own toy robot.

Where do robots fit into your life?

The Honda ASIMO is a humanoid robot.

How robots work

Building working robots is a complex job. Scientists and engineers work together to develop the most useful systems. This book looks at how robots actually work, including:

- huge robots that work in car factories
- robotic cranes that shift enormous loads from ships
- robotic explorers that roll across the surface of Mars

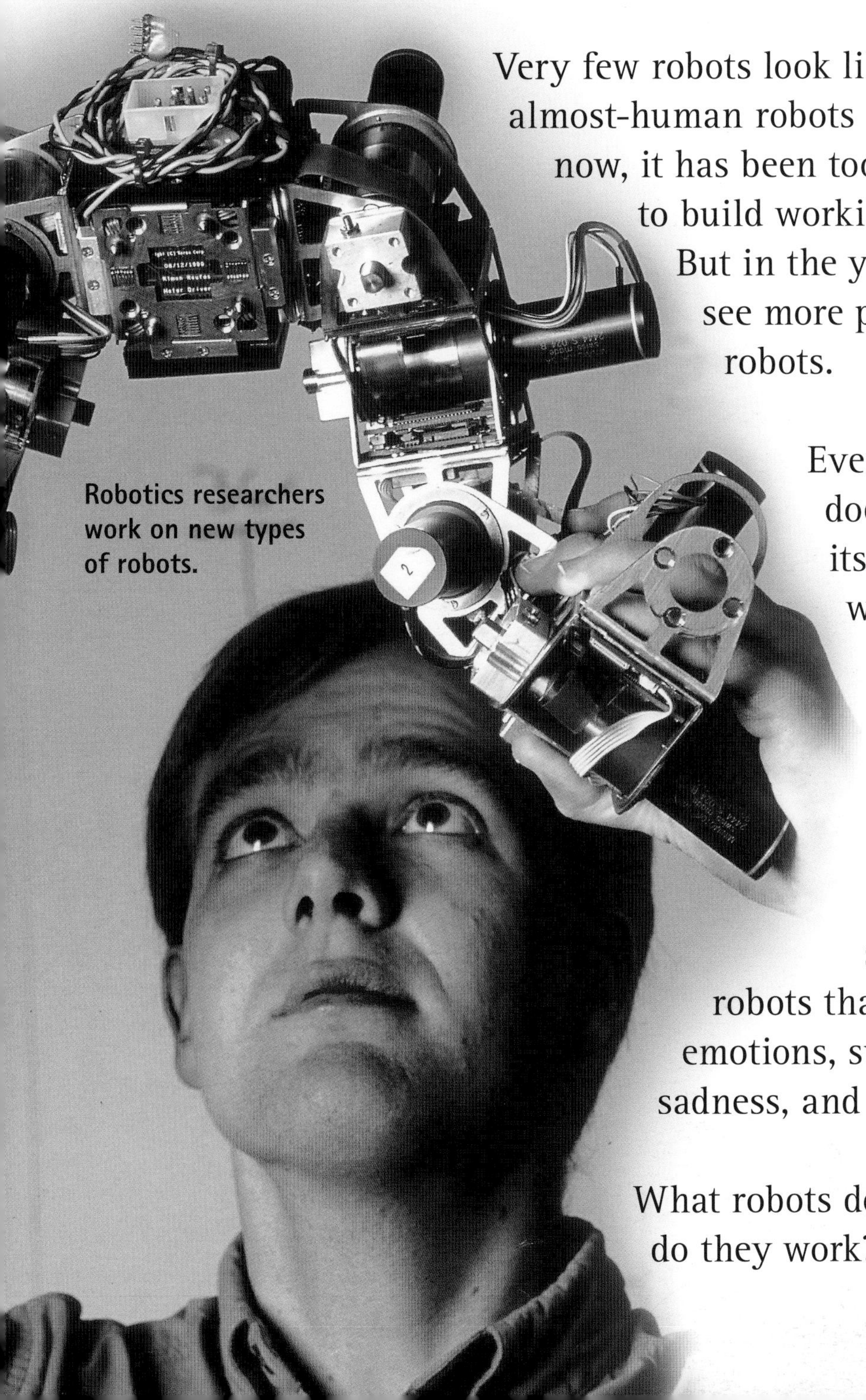

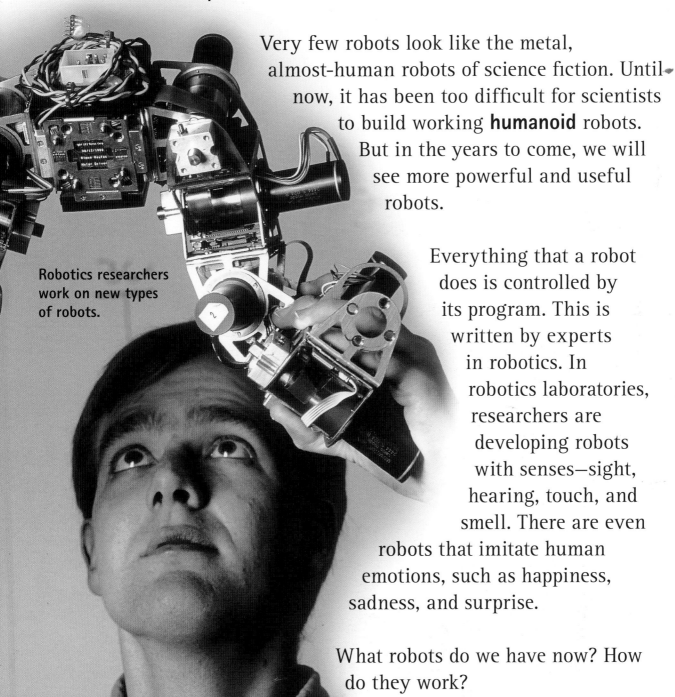

Robotics researchers work on new types of robots.

Very few robots look like the metal, almost-human robots of science fiction. Until now, it has been too difficult for scientists to build working **humanoid** robots. But in the years to come, we will see more powerful and useful robots.

Everything that a robot does is controlled by its program. This is written by experts in robotics. In robotics laboratories, researchers are developing robots with senses—sight, hearing, touch, and smell. There are even robots that imitate human emotions, such as happiness, sadness, and surprise.

What robots do we have now? How do they work?

What is a robot?

A robot is a machine that has some intelligence. It can move and do certain jobs. But robots cannot work entirely by themselves. Humans control robots by programming their actions using computers. Computers are not robots, though they form a part of every robot.

Robots can perform jobs that are impossible for humans. They can:
- dive to the bottom of the ocean
- explore a volcano
- repair a damaged **nuclear reactor**

Other robots do jobs that are boring and repetitive. Thousands of robotic arms work in car factories. They **weld** metal, spray paint, or tighten bolts. Unlike humans, robots can work in factories 24 hours a day, seven days a week. They are never bored or tired.

ROBOFACT

WHY DO WE CALL THEM "ROBOTS"?

The word "robot" comes from the Czech word *robota*, which means "hard work." The Czech writer Karel Capek first used "robot" in a play in 1920.

Robotic arms are the most common of all robots.

Underwater robots, such as Hercules, can be used to explore deep in the ocean.

Types of robots

Some robots look a bit like humans. They walk on two legs and have two arms. They peer at the world with two eyes in an almost-human face.

Other robots roll around on wheels or on **caterpillar tracks**. There is nothing human about these robots. They can roll across burning deserts, or deep into buildings damaged by an earthquake. Their powerful wheels or tracks can take them almost anywhere.

Under the sea, robots explore sunken ships or collect samples from the ocean floor. Robotic planes and helicopters fly overhead. They can stay in the air for hours.

The smallest robots are no bigger than insects. They scuttle on many legs like cockroaches, or fly using wings. The largest robots are huge mine shovels that pick up tons of coal in every scoop.

Whatever their size or shape, robots are all made for one thing. They all do work.

Movement

Robots need to be able to move to do their work. Some robots are simply a moving arm, while others are far more complex.

Robotic arm

The simplest working robot is the robotic arm. It is firmly bolted to the factory floor, but it can still move by bending and twisting.

Degrees of freedom

Engineers describe a robot's movements as **degrees of freedom** (DOF). A robotic arm with one hinged joint has one degree of freedom. A modern **industrial** robot can turn at the waist. It can move at the shoulder, elbow, and wrist. This gives it six degrees of freedom.

Tools

Industrial robotic arms are fitted with a particular tool for each job. In a car factory, some robots have drills. Others have tools that fit bolts, or weld sections of the car together.

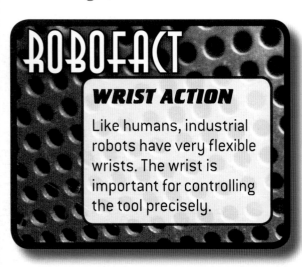

ROBOFACT

WRIST ACTION

Like humans, industrial robots have very flexible wrists. The wrist is important for controlling the tool precisely.

Robotic arms stay in one spot, repeating one task over and over.

Controlling the robot

Robots are controlled by a computer program. This is a long list of very exact instructions for the computer to follow.

Computer programs for an industrial robot are difficult to write correctly. They have to give the robot the correct instructions. The programs are written by computer engineers who are experts in robotics.

The computer program is stored in the robot's computer memory. If it needs to be changed, the engineer can read it and correct it on a computer.

Making programming easier

Programming for simple robots, such as Lego robots or Aibo robotic dogs, is much easier. The programmer can choose a set of program **icons** to drag onto a screen. Each icon describes a part of the robot's movement. Using the correct commands, the programmer can make the Lego robot or Aibo dog do anything within its ability.

A programmer plans the actions of an industrial robot.

Wheeled robots

Most robots move around on wheels or caterpillar tracks. Wheels support the robot easily and don't need complicated machinery to move. They keep the robot well balanced, so it doesn't tip over. When the robot comes to rough ground, it can roll straight over it.

Large-wheeled robots

The Martian **rovers** roll along on six large, independent wheels. Each wheel has its own motor and its own suspension. When the rover comes to rocky ground, its wheels roll straight up and over the rocks.

Small-wheeled robots

Small-wheeled robots such as iRobot's Roomba work as cleaners. These robots roll around on smooth floors and carpet while they do their work.

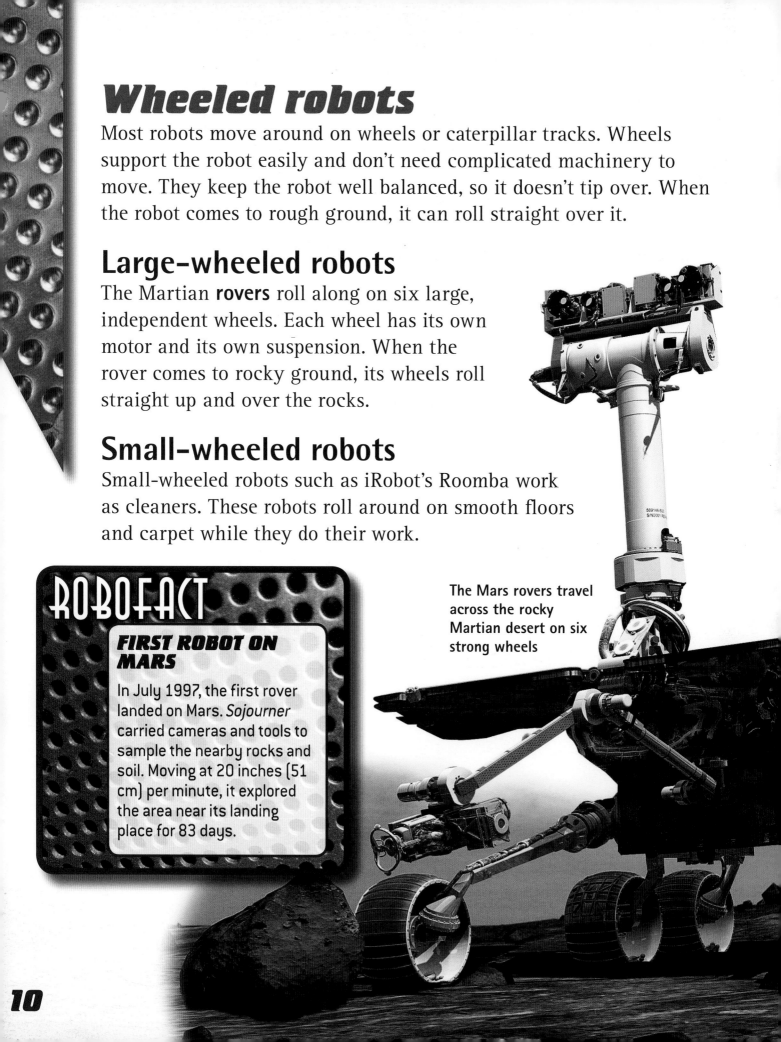

The Mars rovers travel across the rocky Martian desert on six strong wheels

ROBOFACT

FIRST ROBOT ON MARS

In July 1997, the first rover landed on Mars. *Sojourner* carried cameras and tools to sample the nearby rocks and soil. Moving at 20 inches (51 cm) per minute, it explored the area near its landing place for 83 days.

PackBot, a small tracked robot, is often used for exploring.

Tracked robots

Vehicles with caterpillar tracks, such as tanks and bulldozers, can drive over very rough areas. Tracks work much better than wheels, as they cannot get stuck in holes or behind rocks. Researchers used this idea to develop robots that could climb stairs or drive across open land.

Bomb disposal robots

Bomb disposal robots usually have caterpillar tracks. Bomb disposal experts stay at a safe distance, guiding the robot by remote control. The robots can travel into buildings, up and down stairs, until they find the bomb.

Soldiers have used tracked robots to search deep inside caves in Afghanistan. The robots can travel into places where it is not safe for soldiers to go. They send back video and sound so that the soldiers can tell if the area is safe.

The same tracked robots were used to explore the ruins of the World Trade Center when it was destroyed on September 11, 2001.

How many legs?

How many legs does a robot need? A robot with many legs is more stable than a two-legged robot. If one leg cannot find a steady position, the other legs still support the robot.

Six-legged robots

Researchers studied how insects walk to develop a six-legged robot, called Elma. Each of its legs has a tiny, computer-controlled motor. The robot scuttles forward like a cockroach, moving three legs at a time.

Eight-legged robots

The eight-legged robot Dante II was used to explore a volcano in 1994. For five days Dante performed well, until it fell over and was unable to get upright again. Today, researchers know that a robot with many legs needs to be able to get up without human help.

ROBOFACT

A ROBOT AT THE BEACH

Ariel is a crab-like robot. It can crawl around beaches and in shallow water. It is designed to hunt for unexploded bombs in wartime.

Ariel is designed to walk like a crab in shallow water.

Up Close

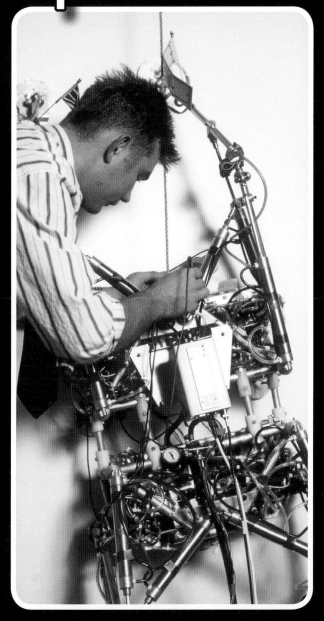

ROBOT
Robug

JOB
Hazardous duties

MAKER
University of Portsmouth, England

SKILLS
Climbing walls, pulling heavy loads

SIZE
30 inches (76 cm) long,
24 inches (61 cm) wide,
24 inches (61 cm) high

SPECIAL FEATURES
Built-in video cameras, suction pads

Robug is an experimental robot. It has eight 39-inch (99 cm) legs, so it walks like a huge spider or a crab. It can climb into dangerous areas, such as damaged nuclear reactors.

Operators guide Robug from a safe distance. They use the robot's built-in cameras to see where it is going. But Robug works out its own walking movement. It can walk over rough and broken ground. Like a crab, it always has several feet supporting it on firm ground.

Robug's special suction pads allow it to climb walls like a spider. It is very strong, and can drag a 220-pound (100 kg) load along the ground. Several Robug robots have been developed. The latest is Robug IV.

Senses

How does a robot sense the world around it? Most robots can "see" and "hear," and robots usually need a sense of touch. Very few robots have a sense of taste or of smell.

Some robots uses light sensors to follow a visible trail.

Sense of sight

Robot sight is quite different from human sight. Humans automatically recognize hundreds of items, such as chairs and tables. But for a robot, the world is a blur of colors and shapes.

Robots can be programmed to recognize certain objects. But the robot will not recognize anything that is new, or out of place.

Camera eyes

Many robots do not actually see. Their "eyes" are video cameras that send information back to a human controller. The controller watches where the robot is going and guides it.

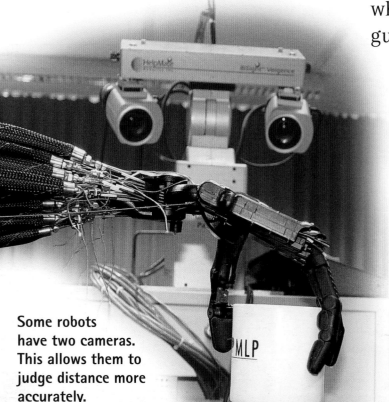

Some robots have two cameras. This allows them to judge distance more accurately.

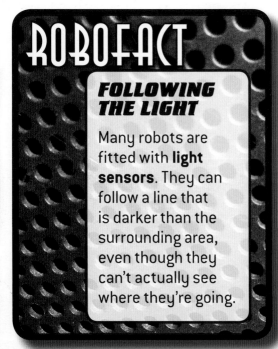

ROBOFACT

FOLLOWING THE LIGHT

Many robots are fitted with **light sensors**. They can follow a line that is darker than the surrounding area, even though they can't actually see where they're going.

Sense of hearing

Robots detect sound in different ways. Some robots use **ultrasonic sensors** to detect objects. Others can "hear" a human voice. Advanced robots can understand human words and reply.

The small robots called SwarmBot cooperate in a swarm, like a group of ants. They detect each other using sound sensors.

Sonar

Bats and dolphins use **sonar** to find their way around. They send out high-pitched squeaks or clicks, and listen as the sound echoes back to them.

Many robots also use sonar like this. If the sound bounces back quickly, the robot knows there is something in the way. It can turn to avoid the obstacle.

Making conversation

There are no robots yet that are advanced enough to have a conversation with a human. However, some can react to a voice. Kismet, a **face-bot** developed at the Massachusetts Institute of Technology, will turn to hear a voice. It also makes noises that sound like speech.

SwarmBot is a team of robots that use sound sensors to work together.

Sense of touch

It is important for most robots to have a sense of touch. Most working robots need to pick up and put down objects, such as car parts or tools. They must be able to squeeze at the right pressure. Too loose, and they will drop the item; too hard, and they could crush it.

Pressure-sensitive pads

Engineers have developed **pressure-sensitive pads** for robots. These allow the robot to detect just how much pressure it is using. Then, the robot needs to be able to instantly stop squeezing. This level of control is difficult to achieve. The robot's grip is controlled by tiny electric motors, which need to stop instantly.

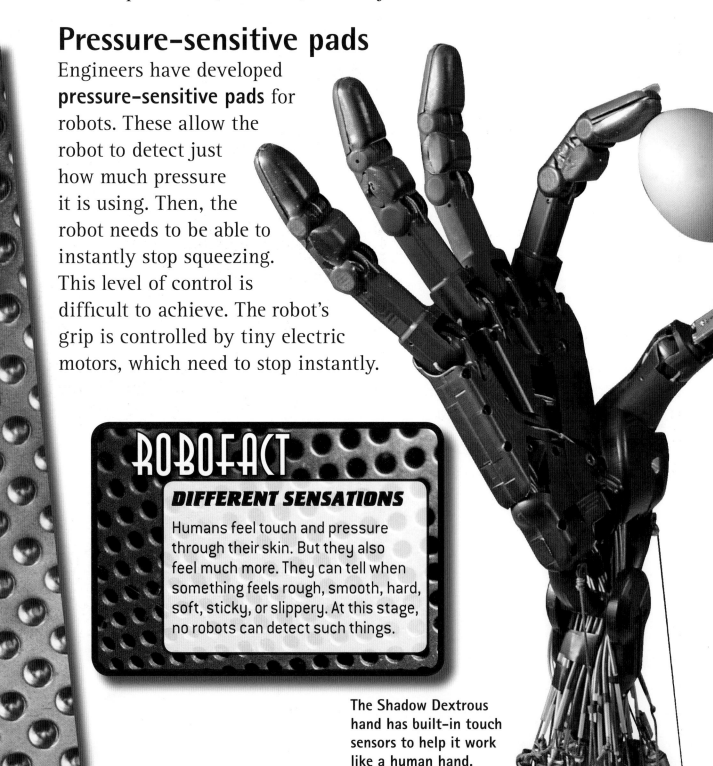

ROBOFACT

DIFFERENT SENSATIONS

Humans feel touch and pressure through their skin. But they also feel much more. They can tell when something feels rough, smooth, hard, soft, sticky, or slippery. At this stage, no robots can detect such things.

The Shadow Dextrous hand has built-in touch sensors to help it work like a human hand.

Sense of smell

Robots that can detect smells may one day work with airport security guards. They can be programmed to search for different smells on different jobs. They could find drugs, chemicals, or even poisonous gases.

Dogs are often trained to do this job now. But unlike robots, dogs need food and shelter. Even the best dogs sometimes follow an interesting smell instead of doing their job!

A RAT that smells

Australian researcher Andy Russell has developed a robot that can detect smells. His RAT (Reactive Autonomous Testbed) follows a trail of scent. It also has ultrasonic sensors to keep it from bumping into walls. It has a set of whiskers as touch sensors.

Andy Russell's RAT robot can follow a trail of scent.

Russell predicts that one day robots using this technology will take over for dogs. Security staff will simply program the smelling sections of the robot. They can program it to search for drugs, weapons, or poisonous gases.

Artificial intelligence

Robots need to be able to think and act without humans controlling them. This ability is called artificial intelligence.

Intelligence is the ability to understand the world around us, and deal with it successfully. People and animals are intelligent. They can think and act independently. If something goes wrong, or a situation changes, they can work out the best actions to take.

Robot intelligence

Robots do not have brains. They rely on programs that tell them how to do certain tasks. Even the most advanced robots can only do the job they are programmed to do. They cannot change their programming, or do a task they have not been programmed for.

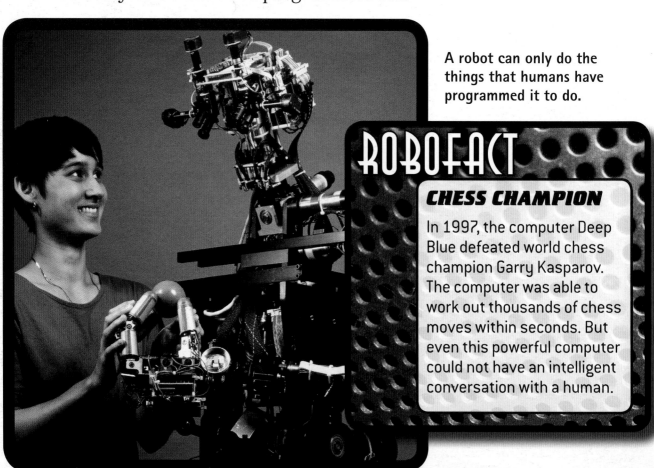

A robot can only do the things that humans have programmed it to do.

ROBOFACT

CHESS CHAMPION

In 1997, the computer Deep Blue defeated world chess champion Garry Kasparov. The computer was able to work out thousands of chess moves within seconds. But even this powerful computer could not have an intelligent conversation with a human.

Up Close

ROBOT
Cog

JOB
Learning robot

MAKER
MIT Artificial Intelligence Lab

SKILLS
Learning about the world

SIZE
Upper body, head, and arms the size of a human

SPECIAL FEATURES
Four built-in cameras, sound sensors, arms with hands and fingers

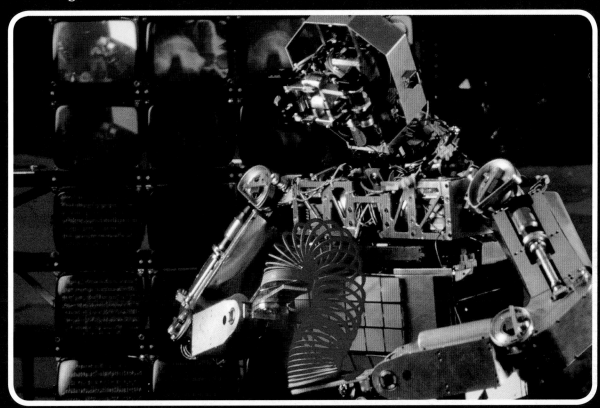

Cog is a robot at the Massachusetts Institute of Technology (MIT). The researchers there try to teach Cog how to recognize things and react to them.

Human babies learn by seeing, hearing, and touching things around them. Researchers at MIT are trying to develop robots that learn in the same way.

Cog can look at objects, then pick them up to look more closely. Its sensors can tell where a sound is coming from. It can make eye contact with humans, and watch objects as they move.

Cog does not have one large computer, but several smaller ones. Each computer controls a different part of its behavior.

Feelings

Humans can feel happy or sad, bored, angry, or afraid. Does a robot need to have feelings like this?

Many researchers think humans would prefer robots that seemed more human. A robot that seems friendly and happy to see us might be better to work with than an emotionless piece of machinery.

Kismet, the "feelings" robot

One of the first robots designed to show feelings was the face-bot Kismet. Kismet's face looks only slightly human. However, its eyes, eyebrows, eyelids, lips, and ears can all move to show emotions. Kismet can seem happy, sad, angry, or even surprised.

Kismet is only a research project in a laboratory. But other robots have now been built that use some of Kismet's research to create realistic faces.

Kismet appears to show human feelings, such as happiness and surprise.

ROBOFACT

LEGO WITH FEELINGS

Even a Lego robot can be programmed to show feelings. Feelix is a Lego robot that can show happiness, anger, or fear when someone touches its feet.

A human face

The most recent robots with feelings all have skin to cover the mechanical parts of their faces. David Hanson, a U.S. researcher, has developed several face-bots.

Each robot's eyes, eyebrows, and lips move as if they are showing emotion. The mouth moves realistically as the robot speaks.

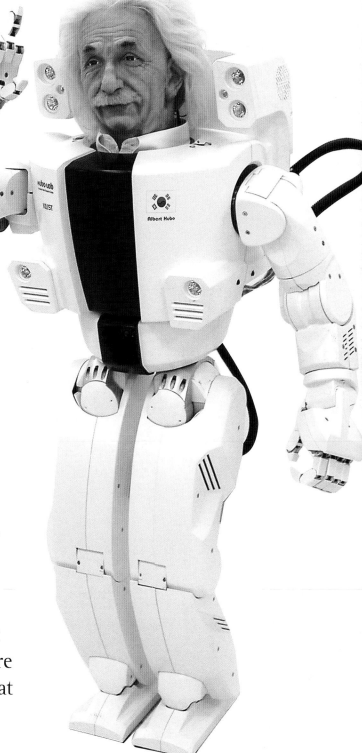

The Albert Einstein robot, from Hanson Robotics, has a very realistic face.

The Albert Einstein robot

One of Hanson's robots is Albert, a robot that looks like Albert Einstein, a famous scientist. Albert's head is mounted on a walking robot. The whole machine is able to move around a room, speaking. Albert's big bushy eyebrows and moustache even move to match his expressions.

Are we ready for a robot that looks this human? Some researchers believe we are more comfortable with robots that do not look like us. They say that most people are actually uncomfortable seeing a robot that seems almost, but not quite, human.

Humanoid robots

Most people's first idea of a robot is of a two-legged machine that looks very much like a human. We call these robots "humanoid."

The movie *Star Wars* gave us C-3PO, the gleaming golden humanoid robot. But there were many metal robots in movies and science fiction magazines before that.

Humanoid robots would fit in well with our human society. They could climb stairs, open doors, and use tables and chairs.

However, humanoid robots are difficult to create. The major problem is teaching them to balance. Humans can stand on two legs because we have natural balancing systems. Humanoid robots find standing upright difficult and tend to fall over easily.

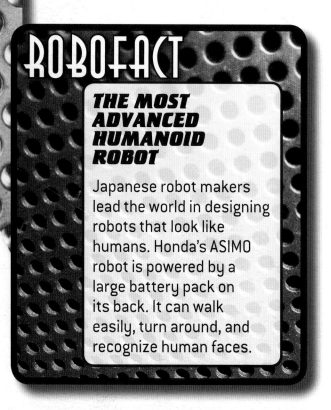

ROBOFACT

THE MOST ADVANCED HUMANOID ROBOT

Japanese robot makers lead the world in designing robots that look like humans. Honda's ASIMO robot is powered by a large battery pack on its back. It can walk easily, turn around, and recognize human faces.

The Honda ASIMO is the world's most advanced humanoid robot.

Up Close

ROBOT
Qrio

JOB
Entertainment robot

MAKER
Sony Corporation, Japan

SKILLS
Walking, running, jumping, and dancing

SIZE
16 inches (40 cm) tall

WEIGHT
115 pounds (52 kg)

Qrio (pronounced "curio") is a small robot, no taller than the average person's waist. But Qrio can move as no other robot has been able to move.

Qrio is able to walk quickly, balancing itself just as humans do. It can dance, swinging and swaying and tapping its feet.

But the most surprising thing about Qrio is that it can run like a human. When people run, there are moments when both their feet are off the ground. Humans are able to stay balanced and keep running. Qrio can run like this as well. Its built-in sensors keep it steady and balanced as it lands.

Qrio is even smart enough to recognize voices and faces.

Most robots in the world do dirty, boring, or dangerous jobs. Factory robots assemble cars and other goods. Huge mining robots scoop up tons of earth. Robotic cranes and trucks work to unload containers from ships.

Factory work

The earliest working robot was Unimate, built in 1961. It had one arm with two joints and a gripper. It stacked hot metal plates in a factory.

Today, car factories use more robots than any other industry. Robots weld and assemble car parts, moving in very precise actions that humans have programmed.

These robots work behind strong steel cages. They have no awareness of anything except their task, and could easily crush a worker who was in the way.

Each robot on an assembly line has one small job to do over and over.

ROBOFACT

CHOCOLATE FACTORY ROBOTS

Not all working robots do heavy work. In chocolate factories, robots pick up each chocolate and place it carefully into a box. And they never feel like eating a few!

Loading and unloading containers

The port of Rotterdam, in the Netherlands, is the world's busiest sea port. Every day, dozens of huge ships come to load or unload their cargo. It is robots that make this possible.

Robotic cranes and trucks

The port of Rotterdam has 83 massive robotic cranes. These roll along steel tracks, picking up containers and carrying them to robotic trucks. There are more than 140 robotic trucks, known as automated guided vehicles (AGVs). They carry the containers to other parts of the port.

Robotic trucks in the port of Rotterdam move containers from place to place.

The humans who control this system mainly work in control rooms, or in the cabins of the cranes. They do not drive the machinery. They simply tell the robotic cranes and trucks which job to work on next.

The robotic trucks and cranes move along their paths without any human help. They have built-in **guidance sensors** to make sure that they never crash into another vehicle.

Toy robots

The earliest toy robots, made in the 1930s, were simply wind-up tin toys. They looked like robots, but could not do anything except roll along. Toys that could talk, play, and obey commands would have seemed impossible to earlier generations of children.

Battery-powered robots

By the 1960s, toy robots had improved. Battery-powered robots walked and talked, and had flashing lights and moving gears. However, they could still not react to their owners in any way.

Robotic toys

Now, robotic toys are common. Programmable robots, such as the Aibo robotic dog, can do things the earliest toys could never do. They explore their area, show emotions, and even dance. Their owners can interact with them. Owners can program the robots using simple programming languages.

ROBOFACT

BABY DOLL ROBOT

Rodney Brooks, who designed Kismet, developed one of the first lifelike doll robots. This doll looked like a living human baby. It could show 15 human-like emotions.

Old-style tin robot toys were not as realistic as modern robot toys.

Toy robot kits

The real revolution in toy robots was the development of robot kits such as Lego's Mindstorms series. These kits consist of a rectangular "brick" that contains the computer and the power supply. They have a range of lights, wheels, sensors and extra parts.

Robot soccer

Soon, college students realized that they could build Lego robots that could play soccer. They started an international robot soccer competition, known as Robocup. Teams of robots chase a special ball that sends out infrared signals.

Toy robot competitions

The Robocup competition now has a junior section for elementary and high school students. Teams from around the world meet every year to discover which team has the smartest robots.

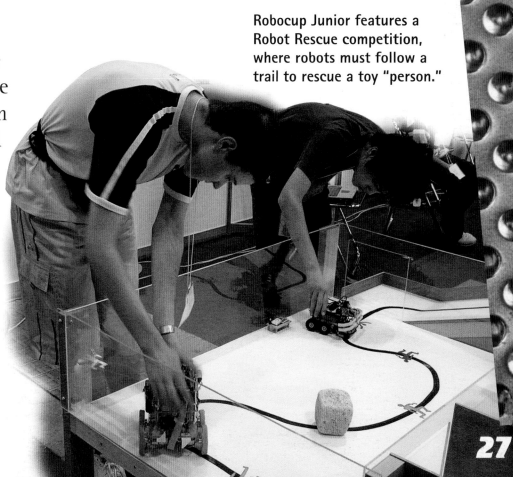

Robocup Junior features a Robot Rescue competition, where robots must follow a trail to rescue a toy "person."

Other robots join in the competition as well. The robot dance competition has robots programmed to dance to music. The robot rescue simulates a real robotic rescue. There is even an Aibo League, in which teams of Aibos play soccer.

27

Future robots

If robots continue to improve, what will we see next? Robots will certainly become smarter. Robotic sensors will improve, so robots will be better able to find their way around.

Household robots

We may see more working robots in our homes. Will they be humanoid, vacuuming or washing the dishes? Or will they just be a box on wheels, rolling around the house cleaning up?

Nanobots

Some scientists predict that we will develop **nanobots**. These machines would be no bigger than the width of a human hair. They could work invisibly, keeping our environment clean. Nanobots could even swim through a person's bloodstream, destroying germs.

ROBOFACT

ROBOT CARS

Robotic cars could make car accidents a thing of the past. Researchers predict that cars of the future will be automatic. We will tell the car where we want to go, and it will take us there, keeping a safe distance from all other vehicles.

Robots will become a part of our daily lives in years to come.

Robot intelligence

Will robots become more intelligent? Is it possible that one day we will create robots that are smarter than humans?

Scientists disagree on this idea. Some say our brains are too complex. They believe that no robots would ever be able to think and act like a human. Other scientists point to how quickly computers have developed over the past 50 years. They predict that, eventually, robots will develop true artificial intelligence.

Part human and part robot?

Scientists such as Ray Kurzweil predict that one day we will become part human and part robot. He believes that humans will use robotic systems as parts of their bodies, replacing body parts with robotic parts that are better and stronger. He says that humans could even improve their brainpower by adding computers.

Could such a thing happen? Do people want it to happen, or would it be better to remain fully human?

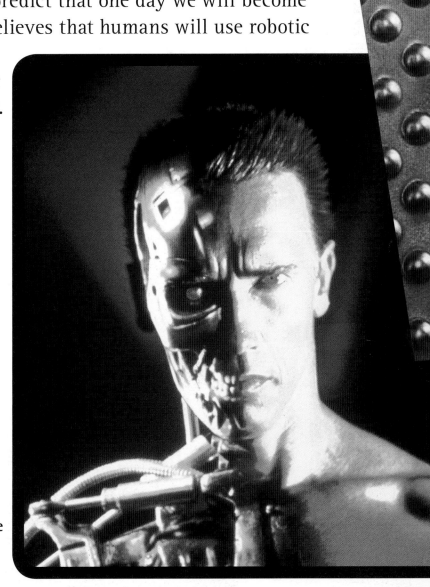

A cyborg is part human, part robot. Could this be a robot of the future?

Program a robot

Robots can't simply work things out, as humans do. Programmers need to give them instructions for every move they make. The instructions are stored in the robot's computer.

See how tricky this can be. Ask a friend to act as a robot for you, following your instructions. Write a program to make your "robot" pick up an object from the other side of the room. List every step, such as:

- move forward
- stop
- turn left
- turn right
- extend arm
- open fingers
- close fingers

Did you need to repeat some steps several times? Did you leave out any important steps? Can you change the program to make it work better?

If you write programs that work well, you could be a robot programmer in the future.

Have fun!

Glossary

bomb disposal - disarming and removing bombs

caterpillar tracks - large tracks used on tanks, bulldozers, and robots so they can travel across rough ground

degrees of freedom - the number of places and directions in which a robotic arm can move

disarm - to make an unexploded bomb safe

face-bot - a robot designed to show natural expressions on a human-like face

guidance sensors - electronic devices that help control a robot's movement

humanoid - similar in shape to a human

icons - pictures or images used to represent a computer program command

industrial - used in a factory

light sensors - electronic devices that detect and measure levels of light

nanobots - tiny robots so small that they are measured in nanometers, or millionths of a millimeter

nuclear reactor - a machine which contains and controls nuclear energy

pressure-sensitive pads - pads with sensors that can detect touch or pressure

program - to install the instructions that control a robot's actions

rovers - robots designed to explore the surface of another planet

science fiction - stories based on futuristic scientific ideas

sonar - a system that uses sound and echoes to detect objects

surgical robots - robots capable of performing surgical operations

ultrasonic sensors - electronic devices that detect and measure sounds that are too high for humans to hear

weld - to join pieces of metal by heating the edges so they melt together

Index